KRISHNA MOHAN AVANCHA

Google: Lead Generation from
Paid to Organic

Contents

1

Understanding Google's Role in Lead Generation

As a digital marketer, I understand that lead generation is the backbone of any business, big or small. It's the process of identifying and cultivating potential customers for your products or services. And when it comes to lead generation, Google plays a crucial role. With over 90% of all online searches happening on Google, it's important to understand how the search engine giant can help you generate leads.

Let's dive into the topic and explore Google's role in lead generation.

1. Google Search Ads:

Google Search Ads are one of the most effective ways to generate leads. These ads appear at the top of the search engine results page (SERP) when users search for specific keywords. You can create ads that target specific keywords and audiences, making sure that your ad is shown to people who are looking for your product or service.

One of the biggest advantages of Google Search Ads is that they are highly targeted. This means that you can show your ad to people who are most likely to convert into customers. You can also set a budget for your ad campaign and pay only when someone clicks on your ad.

1. Google Display Ads:

Google Display Ads are another powerful tool for lead generation. These ads appear on websites that are part of the Google Display Network, which includes millions of websites across the internet. Display ads are usually in the form of banners, images, or videos and are placed on websites that are relevant to your target audience.

Display ads can be targeted based on a number of factors, such as demographics, interests, and website content. This means that you can show your ads to people who are most likely to be interested in your product or service. Display ads can also be retargeted to people who have already visited your website, increasing the chances of converting them into customers.

1. Google My Business:

Google My Business (GMB) is a free tool that allows you to manage your business information on Google. When someone searches for your business on Google, they will see a knowledge panel on the right-hand side of the search results. This panel displays your business information, such as your address, phone number, and business hours.

By optimizing your GMB profile, you can increase your

visibility on Google and generate more leads. Make sure that your business information is accurate and up-to-date, and add photos and videos to showcase your products or services. You can also use GMB to respond to customer reviews, which can help build trust and credibility with potential customers.

1. Google Reviews:

Google Reviews are an important factor in lead generation. When someone searches for your business on Google, they will see a rating and reviews from customers who have used your product or service. Positive reviews can increase your credibility and encourage potential customers to choose your business over your competitors.

To generate more reviews, you can encourage your customers to leave feedback on your Google My Business profile. You can also respond to reviews, both positive and negative, to show that you value your customers' feedback and are committed to providing excellent customer service.

1. Google Analytics:

Google Analytics is a free tool that allows you to track and analyze your website traffic. By understanding how people are finding and using your website, you can make data-driven decisions to improve your lead generation efforts.

With Google Analytics, you can track metrics such as the number of visitors to your website, the pages they visit, and how long they stay on your site. You can also track where your website traffic is coming from, such as organic search, social media, or paid advertising.

By analyzing this data, you can identify areas for improvement and make changes to your website to increase conversions. For example, if you notice that visitors are leaving your website after only a few seconds, you may need to improve your website's design or content to keep them engaged.

2

The Advantages and Disadvantages of Paid Google Ads

As a digital marketer with years of experience, I can attest to the fact that Google Ads (formerly known as Google AdWords) is one of the most powerful tools in the arsenal of any online marketer. It allows businesses to reach their target audience at the precise moment they are searching for specific products or services. But like any marketing strategy, there are advantages and disadvantages to using paid Google Ads.

Advantages of Paid Google Ads

- Instant Visibility

One of the most significant advantages of Google Ads is that it provides instant visibility to your target audience. With Google Ads, your ads can appear at the top of the search engine results page (SERP) when someone searches for relevant keywords. This means that you can start generating traffic and leads immediately, rather than waiting for your SEO efforts to kick in.

- Targeted Reach

Google Ads allows you to target your ads to specific audiences based on a range of factors, such as geographic location, language, device type, and more. This means that you can ensure that your ads are being shown to the right people at the right time, increasing the chances of conversions.

- Measurable Results

With Google Ads, you can track your campaigns' performance and measure your return on investment (ROI) accurately. Google provides a range of metrics, such as click-through rates (CTR), conversion rates, and cost per click (CPC), that allow you to understand how your campaigns are performing and make adjustments as needed.

- Cost-Effective

One of the most significant advantages of Google Ads is that it is cost-effective. You only pay for the clicks your ads receive, which means that you are not wasting money on advertising to people who are not interested in your products or services.
Disadvantages of Paid Google Ads

- Cost

While Google Ads can be cost-effective, it can also be expensive if you are not careful. The cost per click (CPC) for popular keywords can be high, and if you are not monitoring your campaigns regularly, you could end up spending a lot of money without seeing the desired results.

• Competition

As more businesses recognize the value of Google Ads, competition for popular keywords and phrases has become increasingly fierce. This means that it can be challenging to achieve a high ranking for your ads, and you may need to bid higher than your competitors to ensure that your ads are seen.

• Ad Fatigue

Ad fatigue is a common issue with Google Ads. If you are targeting the same audience with the same ad repeatedly, they may become immune to your message, and your ads may lose their effectiveness. This means that you need to be constantly updating and refreshing your ads to keep them engaging and relevant.

• Limited Control

While Google Ads provides a range of targeting options, there are some limitations. For example, you cannot target users based on their income or social status, which can limit your ability to reach certain segments of your target audience.

Conclusion

Google Ads is a powerful tool that can help businesses generate leads and drive sales. However, it is important to understand the advantages and disadvantages of using paid

Google Ads to make informed decisions about whether it is the right marketing strategy for your business. If you decide to use Google Ads, it is essential to have a well-planned and well-executed campaign that is constantly monitored and optimized to ensure that you are getting the most out of your advertising budget.

3

Developing a Google Ads Strategy for Lead Generation

I n the world of digital marketing, Google Ads is one of the most effective ways to generate leads and drive conversions for businesses of all sizes. However, developing a successful Google Ads strategy requires more than just creating a few ad campaigns and hoping for the best. To truly succeed with Google Ads, you need to have a well-thought-out strategy that is tailored to your business goals, target audience, and budget.

In this article, we will outline the key steps you should take when developing a Google Ads strategy for lead generation, including conducting research, defining your target audience, setting goals, selecting the right keywords, creating compelling ad copy, and measuring your results.

Conduct research

Before you begin developing your Google Ads strategy, you need to conduct thorough research to understand your target audience and competition. You should identify your key competitors and examine their ad campaigns to see what is working well and what can be improved upon. Additionally, you should use tools like Google Keyword Planner and Google Trends to identify the keywords and search terms that are most relevant to your business.

Define your target audience

Once you have conducted research, you need to define your target audience. You should identify the demographics, interests, and behaviors of your ideal customer, and use this information to create targeted ad campaigns that speak directly to them. By targeting your ads to a specific audience, you can increase the likelihood that they will engage with your ad and take action.

Set goals

The next step in developing a Google Ads strategy is to set clear goals. You should determine what specific actions you want your audience to take after seeing your ad, whether that is filling out a contact form, signing up for a newsletter, or making a purchase. By setting specific goals, you can measure the success of your ad campaigns and make adjustments as needed.

Select the right keywords

Keywords are a critical component of any Google Ads strategy. You should select keywords that are relevant to your business and that your target audience is likely to search for. Additionally, you should use negative keywords to exclude search terms that are not relevant to your business. This will help ensure that your ads are only shown to people who are most likely to be interested in your product or service.

Create compelling ad copy

Once you have selected your keywords, you need to create compelling ad copy that will entice your audience to click through to your website. Your ad copy should be concise, clear, and focused on the benefits of your product or service. Additionally, you should use a strong call-to-action to encourage your audience to take action.

Measure your results

Finally, it is essential to measure the results of your Google Ads campaigns. You should use tools like Google Analytics to track conversions, click-through rates, and other key metrics. By analyzing this data, you can determine which ad campaigns are most effective and make adjustments as needed to optimize your results.

In addition to these key steps, there are a few best practices that you should keep in mind when developing your Google Ads strategy:

- Use ad extensions: Ad extensions can be used to provide additional information about your business, such as phone numbers, addresses, and links to specific pages on your website. This can help increase the relevance and effectiveness of your ads.
- Test multiple ad variations: You should create multiple ad variations to test different messaging, headlines, and images. By testing multiple ad variations, you can determine which ad elements are most effective and optimize your ads for better results.
- Monitor your budget: You should monitor your Google Ads budget closely to ensure that you are getting the best return on your investment. If an ad campaign is not performing well, you should adjust your budget or pause the campaign altogether.

In conclusion, developing a successful Google Ads strategy for lead generation requires careful planning, research, and execution.

4

Creating Effective Ad Copy for Google Ads

C reating effective ad copy for Google Ads is an essential part of any successful digital marketing campaign. Google Ads, formerly known as Google AdWords, is a powerful tool that allows businesses to target potential customers with precision and reach a large audience. However, in order to get the most out of your Google Ads campaign, you need to create ad copy that is effective and compelling.

As a digital marketer with years of experience in creating effective ad copy for Google Ads, I have developed several strategies that can help you create ads that drive clicks and conversions.

Understand Your Audience

The first step in creating effective ad copy is to understand your audience. Who are you targeting with your ads? What are their needs, interests, and pain points? By understanding your target audience, you can create ad copy that speaks directly to them and addresses their specific needs.

To better understand your audience, conduct research using

tools like Google Analytics and Google Ads' Audience Insights. These tools can help you gather data on your target audience, such as their demographics, interests, and behaviors. You can also conduct surveys or interviews with your existing customers to gain a better understanding of their needs and preferences.

Use Attention-Grabbing Headlines

Your ad headlines are the first thing that potential customers will see when they come across your ad. Therefore, it's important to make sure your headlines are attention-grabbing and compelling. Your headline should clearly communicate what your ad is offering and why it's relevant to the viewer.

To create effective headlines, use power words that evoke emotion and grab attention. Examples of power words include "discover," "proven," "exclusive," and "limited time." You can also use numbers and statistics in your headlines to make your ads more tangible and credible.

Tailor Your Ad Copy to Your Landing Page

Your ad copy should be closely tied to the landing page that it leads to. Make sure your ad copy and landing page have a consistent message and offer. This helps to create a seamless user experience and increases the chances of conversion.

When creating your ad copy, make note of the specific benefits and features of your product or service that you want to highlight. This will help you create ad copy that is tailored to your landing page and that speaks directly to the needs of your audience.

Highlight Your Unique Selling Proposition

Your unique selling proposition (USP) is what sets your product or service apart from your competitors. Your ad copy should highlight your USP and communicate why your product or service is the best choice for your audience.

When highlighting your USP, focus on the benefits that your product or service provides. For example, if you're selling a fitness app, your USP might be that it offers personalized workout plans based on the user's fitness level and goals. In your ad copy, you might highlight the benefits of personalized workouts, such as faster results and a reduced risk of injury.

Include a Clear Call to Action

Your ad copy should include a clear call to action (CTA) that tells the viewer what action to take next. Your CTA should be action-oriented and communicate a sense of urgency. For example, instead of saying "Learn More," you might say "Start Your Free Trial Today" or "Get 50% Off Now."

To create an effective CTA, consider the goals of your campaign and what action you want viewers to take. Do you want them to make a purchase, sign up for a free trial, or download a whitepaper? Make sure your CTA is aligned with your campaign goals and clearly communicates what action the viewer should take.

Test and Optimize Your Ad Copy

Once you've created your ad copy, it's important to test and optimize it to improve its performance.

5

Maximizing Your Google Ads Budget for Lead Generation

As a digital marketer, one of the most important aspects of my job is maximizing my clients' budgets for lead generation. In the world of digital advertising, Google Ads is one of the most powerful tools available for lead generation, and there are several strategies that can be used to ensure that your budget is being spent in the most effective way possible.

- Understand your target audience

The first step in maximizing your Google Ads budget for lead generation is to understand your target audience. Who are they, and what are they looking for? What keywords are they using to search for your products or services? What are their pain points, and how can you address them through your advertising? By answering these questions, you can create ads that speak directly to your target audience and increase the likelihood that they will convert into leads.

- Use the right keywords

Using the right keywords is essential for maximizing your Google Ads budget for lead generation. You want to make sure that your ads are appearing for the keywords that your target audience is using to search for your products or services. This means conducting keyword research and choosing keywords that have a high search volume and low competition. You can also use long-tail keywords, which are more specific and targeted, to increase the likelihood of conversion.

- Create compelling ad copy

Once you have identified your target audience and chosen the right keywords, the next step is to create compelling ad copy. Your ads should be clear, concise, and focused on the benefits of your products or services. Use language that speaks directly to your target audience and addresses their pain points. You can also include a call-to-action that encourages them to take the next step, such as filling out a form or contacting your business.

- Use ad extensions

Ad extensions are a powerful tool for maximizing your Google Ads budget for lead generation. Ad extensions allow you to include additional information in your ads, such as phone numbers, addresses, and links to specific pages on your website. This makes it easier for your target audience to take action and convert into leads. Ad extensions can also increase the visibility and click-through rate of your ads, which can improve your overall ad performance.

- Optimize your landing pages

The landing page is where your target audience will go after clicking on your ad, so it's essential to optimize it for lead generation. Your landing page should be focused on the specific product or service that you are advertising and should have a clear call-to-action that encourages visitors to take the next step. You can also include lead capture forms on your landing page to make it easy for visitors to convert into leads.

- Monitor and adjust your campaigns

Monitoring and adjusting your Google Ads campaigns is essential for maximizing your budget for lead generation. You should regularly review your campaigns to see which keywords, ad copy, and landing pages are performing the best. You can then adjust your campaigns accordingly to optimize your budget and improve your results. This may involve pausing underperforming campaigns or shifting your budget to campaigns that are generating the most leads.

- Use remarketing

Remarketing is a powerful strategy for maximizing your Google Ads budget for lead generation. Remarketing allows you to target people who have already visited your website or interacted with your brand in some way. By targeting these people with specific ads, you can increase the likelihood that they will convert into leads. Remarketing can also be used to target people who have abandoned a shopping cart or filled out a lead capture form but did not complete the process.

In conclusion, maximizing your Google Ads budget for lead generation requires a combination of strategies, including understanding your target audience, using the right keywords, creating compelling ad copy, using ad extensions, optimizing your landing pages, monitoring and adjusting your campaigns, and using remarketing.

6

The Power of Google Display Ads for Lead Generation

As a digital marketer with years of experience in lead generation campaigns, I can confidently say that Google Display Ads are one of the most powerful tools available for reaching your target audience and generating leads. Display Ads are an effective way to showcase your brand, products, and services to potential customers while they browse the internet.

Google Display Ads provide marketers with an unparalleled ability to target specific audiences. By using Google's vast data resources, you can target people based on their location, interests, behavior, demographics, and more. This level of granularity allows you to reach people who are most likely to be interested in your products or services and are more likely to convert into leads.

One of the biggest benefits of Google Display Ads is their ability to reach a wide audience. Unlike search ads, which are only shown to people actively searching for specific keywords, display ads are shown to people who are browsing the internet, regardless of whether they are actively searching for your products or services. This means that you can reach a wider audience and increase your chances of generating leads.

Another advantage of Google Display Ads is that they allow you to showcase your brand and products in a visually appealing way. Display Ads can include images, videos, and other multimedia content, which makes them more eye-catching and engaging than text-only search ads. This can help you grab the attention of potential customers and increase their interest in your brand.

One effective way to use Google Display Ads for lead generation is through remarketing campaigns. Remarketing allows you to target people who have already interacted with your brand, such as by visiting your website or signing up for your email list. By targeting people who have already shown an interest in your brand, you can increase your chances of converting them into leads.

Another way to use Google Display Ads for lead generation is by creating custom audiences. Custom audiences allow you to target people who have similar characteristics or behaviors to your existing customers. For example, you can create a custom audience of people who have recently purchased products similar to yours. This can help you reach people who are more likely to be interested in your products or services and increase your chances of generating leads.

One key factor to keep in mind when using Google Display Ads for lead generation is the importance of creating compelling ad content. Your ads need to be visually appealing and grab the attention of your target audience. They also need to clearly communicate the value of your products or services and provide a clear call-to-action (CTA) that encourages people to take the next step, such as filling out a form or contacting your sales team.

It's also important to continually monitor and optimize your Google Display Ads campaigns. This involves analyzing your campaign data, such as click-through rates (CTR), conversion rates, and cost-per-lead (CPL), and making adjustments to improve performance. For example, if you notice that certain ads or targeting options are not performing well, you can adjust your campaign to focus on more effective options.

In conclusion, Google Display Ads are a powerful tool for lead generation. By using the targeting options available through Google, you can reach a highly relevant audience and increase your chances of generating leads. Display Ads also provide a visually appealing way to showcase your brand and products, making them more engaging to potential customers.

7

Leveraging Google Remarketing for Increased Leads

Google Remarketing is a powerful digital marketing tool that can help businesses increase their leads by targeting customers who have previously interacted with their brand. Remarketing allows businesses to target ads to customers who have already shown an interest in their products or services, increasing the likelihood of converting them into paying customers.

Here are some tips for leveraging Google Remarketing for increased leads:

- Set Up Your Remarketing Campaign Correctly

The first step to leveraging Google Remarketing is to ensure that your campaign is set up correctly. This includes creating a remarketing audience, selecting the right ad format, and setting your bid strategy. It is essential to create an audience based on users who have already visited your website or engaged with your brand in some way.

- Create Compelling Ads

Once you have set up your remarketing campaign, it's time to create compelling ads that will attract potential customers. Ads that are eye-catching, well-designed, and personalized to the user's previous interactions with your brand are more likely to convert. Ensure that your ads are optimized for different devices, including mobile, desktop, and tablet.

- Use Dynamic Remarketing

Dynamic Remarketing allows you to create personalized ads that show products or services that customers have previously viewed on your website. This type of remarketing is highly effective as it targets users with specific products they are already interested in. It helps to increase the likelihood of conversion by showing customers products or services they are already considering.

- Test and Refine Your Campaign

As with any digital marketing campaign, it's essential to continuously test and refine your remarketing strategy. Analyze the performance of your ads and adjust your bid strategy, ad format, and targeting accordingly. This can help improve your campaign's performance and increase your return on investment (ROI).

- Leverage Other Google Marketing Tools

Google Remarketing works best when it's integrated with other

Google marketing tools, such as Google Analytics and Google Ads. Google Analytics can help you track user behavior on your website, which can inform your remarketing strategy. Google Ads can help you expand your reach beyond just remarketing, allowing you to target new customers with search and display ads.

In conclusion, leveraging Google Remarketing for increased leads requires proper set-up, compelling ads, dynamic remarketing, testing and refining your campaign, and leveraging other Google marketing tools. By following these tips, businesses can increase their leads and boost their conversion rates. It's essential to keep in mind that remarketing is just one part of an overall digital marketing strategy, and it should be integrated with other marketing channels for the best results.

8

How to Use Google Shopping Ads for Lead Generation

Google Shopping Ads have been traditionally used by eCommerce retailers to showcase their products to potential buyers who are actively searching for similar items on Google. However, this advertising platform can also be used effectively for lead generation.

In this article, I'll guide you through the process of using Google Shopping Ads to generate leads for your business. Here's what we'll cover:

1. Understanding Google Shopping Ads
2. Setting up Google Shopping Ads for lead generation
3. Optimizing your Google Shopping Ads for lead generation

1. Understanding Google Shopping Ads

Google Shopping Ads is an advertising platform that allows retailers to showcase their products in Google search results, Google Images, and Google Shopping. These ads appear at the top of the search results and contain product images, titles, prices, and a brief description.

While these ads are primarily used by eCommerce retailers, they can also be used by businesses looking to generate leads. In this case, instead of promoting specific products, you can use Google Shopping Ads to promote a service or offer.

2. Setting up Google Shopping Ads for lead generation

To set up Google Shopping Ads for lead generation, you'll need to follow these steps:

1. Create a Google Ads account if you haven't already.
2. Link your Google Ads account to your Google Merchant Center account. This will allow you to create product listings for your ads.
3. Create a new campaign in Google Ads and select the "Shopping" campaign type.
4. Create a new ad group within your campaign and set up your targeting. In this case, you'll want to target users who are likely to be interested in your service or offer.
5. Create a product group within your ad group and add your offer or service to the product feed. Make sure to include a clear and concise description of your offer in the product title and description.
6. Set your bids and budget for your campaign.

3. Optimizing your Google Shopping Ads for lead generation

Once you've set up your Google Shopping Ads campaign for lead generation, you'll want to optimize your ads for maximum effectiveness. Here are some tips:

1. Use high-quality images and clear, concise titles and descriptions to attract attention to your ad.
2. Include a call-to-action (CTA) in your ad to encourage users to take action. For example, "Sign up now for a free trial" or "Book your appointment today".
3. Use negative keywords to filter out irrelevant searches and ensure that your ad is shown to the right audience.
4. Test different bidding strategies and ad formats to see what works best for your business.
5. Monitor your ad performance regularly and make adjustments as needed.

In conclusion, Google Shopping Ads can be an effective tool for lead generation, even for businesses that don't sell physical products. By following the steps outlined above and optimizing your ads for maximum effectiveness, you can generate high-quality leads and grow your business.

9

The Pros and Cons of Google's Local Services Ads

As a digital marketer with extensive experience in managing advertising campaigns for businesses of all sizes, I have had the opportunity to work with Google's Local Services Ads (LSAs) and see their impact firsthand. LSAs are a relatively new advertising feature that Google introduced in 2015 to help connect local service providers with potential customers in their area. The ads are displayed at the top of Google search results, above the standard pay-per-click ads and organic search results.

Like any advertising platform, there are both advantages and disadvantages to using Google's Local Services Ads. Here are some of the pros and cons to consider before incorporating LSAs into your digital marketing strategy:

Pros:

1. Increased Visibility: By advertising with Local Services Ads, your business will appear at the top of the search engine results page, increasing your visibility and exposure

to potential customers who are searching for the services you offer.

2. Credibility and Trust: Local Services Ads provide an extra layer of trust and credibility for your business. Your business must undergo a background check and meet Google's quality standards to qualify for the program, and customers can leave reviews of their experiences with your business. These features can help potential customers feel more confident in choosing your business over your competitors.

3. Cost-Effective: Local Services Ads operate on a pay-per-lead model, meaning you only pay when a potential customer contacts you through the ad. This can be more cost-effective than traditional pay-per-click advertising models, where you pay each time someone clicks on your ad, regardless of whether they convert into a customer.

4. Easy Management: The platform is relatively easy to manage, with a simple dashboard that allows you to track your performance, respond to customer inquiries, and manage your budget.

Cons:

1. Limited Availability: Local Services Ads are currently only available for specific service industries and in specific geographic locations. If your business is not in one of these industries or locations, you will not be able to use LSAs.

2. Limited Customization: The platform has limited customization options compared to other advertising platforms, such as Google Ads. You cannot create your own

ad copy, and the ad format is standardized across all businesses in the program.

3. Lower Ad Position: Local Services Ads appear at the top of the search engine results page, but they are placed below Google Ads and above the organic search results. This means that LSAs may receive fewer clicks than Google Ads, which could impact your overall conversion rates.

4. Potential for Fraudulent Activity: There have been instances of fraudulent activity on the platform, where competitors or individuals unrelated to your business may click on your ad to generate false leads and increase your advertising costs.

In conclusion, Local Services Ads can be a valuable addition to your digital marketing strategy if you are in one of the supported service industries and geographic locations. However, it is important to carefully consider the pros and cons before investing in the platform to ensure that it aligns with your business goals and budget. If you do decide to use LSAs, be sure to monitor your performance closely and be aware of any potential fraudulent activity.

10

Optimizing Your Google My Business Profile for Lead Generation

Google My Business is a powerful tool for local businesses to showcase their services and products to potential customers. However, many businesses fail to optimize their Google My Business profiles, leading to missed opportunities for lead generation. In this guide, I'll share some tips on how to optimize your Google My Business profile for lead generation.

1. Claim and verify your Google My Business listing

The first step to optimizing your Google My Business profile is to claim and verify your listing. This ensures that your business information is accurate and up-to-date, and that you can control how your business appears on Google search and maps. To claim your listing, go to Google My Business and follow the prompts to verify your business. This may involve receiving a postcard or phone call from Google with a verification code.

1. Optimize your business information

Once you have claimed and verified your listing, it's time to optimize your business information. Make sure your business name, address, and phone number (NAP) are accurate and consistent across all online platforms. Add a business description that includes relevant keywords and showcases what makes your business unique. Include your business hours, website URL, and photos or videos that showcase your products or services.

1. Encourage customer reviews

Customer reviews are a key factor in how Google ranks local businesses. Encourage your customers to leave reviews on your Google My Business profile by providing excellent service and asking for feedback. Respond to all reviews, both positive and negative, to show that you value your customers' opinions.

1. Use Google My Business messaging

Google My Business now offers a messaging feature that allows customers to contact you directly through your profile. Enable this feature and respond promptly to customer inquiries to increase engagement and generate leads.

1. Post regular updates

Google My Business allows businesses to post updates about their products, services, and events. Take advantage of this feature by posting regular updates that showcase what's new and exciting about your business. Use keywords and hashtags to improve visibility and encourage engagement.

1. Use Google My Business insights

Google My Business provides valuable insights into how customers are finding and interacting with your business on Google. Use this data to identify trends, track your performance, and adjust your strategy accordingly.

By following these tips, you can optimize your Google My Business profile for lead generation and increase your online visibility. Keep in mind that optimizing your profile is an ongoing process, and you should regularly review and update your information to ensure that it remains accurate and up-to-date.

11

The Basics of Google SEO for Lead Generation

As a digital marketer, I understand the importance of search engine optimization (SEO) for lead generation. SEO is the process of optimizing your website to rank higher on search engines like Google. The higher your website ranks, the more likely people are to click on your website and become potential leads. In this article, I will go over the basics of Google SEO for lead generation.

Keyword Research Keyword research is the foundation of SEO. It is the process of identifying the keywords that people use to find information related to your business. Once you have identified these keywords, you can create content that targets these keywords. This content will be more likely to rank on Google and drive traffic to your website.

On-Page SEO On-page SEO refers to the optimization of your website's content and HTML source code. This includes optimizing your title tags, meta descriptions, header tags, and content. By optimizing these elements, you can make your website more appealing to search engines like Google. You

35

should also make sure your website is mobile-friendly and has a fast loading time.

Off-Page SEO Off-page SEO refers to the optimization of external factors that influence your website's ranking. This includes building high-quality backlinks, social media sharing, and guest blogging. Backlinks are links from other websites that point to your website. The more high-quality backlinks you have, the more likely Google is to rank your website higher.

Local SEO Local SEO is important for businesses that want to target customers in their local area. This includes optimizing your Google My Business profile, creating local content, and building local citations. By optimizing your local SEO, you can increase your visibility in Google's local search results and attract more local customers.

Content Marketing Content marketing is the process of creating high-quality content that attracts and engages your target audience. This includes blog posts, videos, infographics, and other types of content. By creating high-quality content that targets your audience's interests, you can attract more traffic to your website and generate more leads.

In conclusion, Google SEO is a crucial part of lead generation. By optimizing your website for search engines like Google, you can increase your visibility, attract more traffic, and generate more leads. This requires a combination of keyword research, on-page and off-page SEO, local SEO, and content marketing. By implementing these strategies, you can improve your website's ranking on Google and attract more potential leads to your business.

12

Conducting Keyword Research for Google SEO

As a digital marketer, conducting effective keyword research is one of the most critical steps to ensure your website ranks well on Google search engine results pages (SERPs). Keyword research involves identifying the right search terms and phrases that potential customers use to find the products, services, or information that your website provides. This process allows you to optimize your website content and improve your visibility in search engine results pages.

Here are some essential steps to follow when conducting keyword research for Google SEO:

- Define Your Objectives

Before you start your keyword research, it's essential to identify your website's goals and objectives. Ask yourself: What do you want to achieve from your website? Do you want to generate more leads, increase sales, or increase brand awareness? Defining your objectives will help you identify the right keywords that align with your business goals.

- Create a List of Relevant Topics

The next step is to create a list of relevant topics that are related to your business. These topics should be broad and cover the key areas that your business operates in. For example, if you run a fitness center, your topics might include "strength training," "cardio workouts," "yoga," and "nutrition."

- Generate a List of Seed Keywords

Once you have a list of relevant topics, it's time to generate a list of seed keywords. Seed keywords are the foundation of your keyword research and will help you identify related search terms and phrases. Use Google's autocomplete feature or a keyword research tool like Google Keyword Planner, Ahrefs, or SEMrush to generate a list of seed keywords.

- Expand Your Keyword List

After generating a list of seed keywords, it's time to expand your keyword list. Use tools like Google Keyword Planner, Ahrefs, or SEMrush to find related keywords and long-tail keywords that are relevant to your business. Long-tail keywords are longer and more specific phrases that people use to search for information. They have less competition and can help you rank higher on Google.

- Analyze Keyword Metrics

Once you have a list of keywords, it's time to analyze their metrics. Look for keywords with a high search volume and low competition. The search volume indicates the number of people searching for a particular keyword, while the competition indicates how difficult it is to rank for that keyword. Aim for keywords with a high search volume and low competition.

• Prioritize Your Keywords

After analyzing the metrics, it's time to prioritize your keywords. Focus on the keywords that are most relevant to your business goals and have the highest potential to drive traffic and conversions. Create a list of primary and secondary keywords that you will use in your website content.

• Monitor Your Keywords

Keyword research is an ongoing process, and you should monitor your keywords regularly. Use tools like Google Search Console, Ahrefs, or SEMrush to track your keyword rankings and identify opportunities for improvement. Update your website content regularly to ensure that it remains relevant and optimized for the keywords that you're targeting.

In conclusion, conducting effective keyword research is essential for Google SEO. By following the steps outlined above, you can identify the right keywords to optimize your website content and improve your visibility in search engine results pages. Remember to monitor your keywords regularly and update your website content to ensure that it remains relevant and optimized for your target keywords.

13

Creating Content that Converts for Google SEO

As a digital marketer with years of experience in search engine optimization (SEO), I understand that creating content that converts for Google SEO is crucial for businesses to attract and retain customers. With Google's constantly evolving algorithm, it's important to develop content that not only ranks well but also encourages users to take action.

To create content that converts for Google SEO, there are several key factors to consider.

• Know Your Target Audience:

Before creating any content, it's important to understand who your target audience is. Conducting in-depth research on your audience's demographics, interests, and pain points will help you create content that resonates with them. Understanding your target audience's search behavior can help you identify keywords and phrases to use in your content.

- Focus on User Intent:

Creating content that aligns with user intent is critical for SEO success. Google aims to deliver search results that satisfy the user's search intent, so it's important to create content that matches their search query. For example, if someone is searching for "best budget laptops," they are likely looking for a list of affordable laptops, not an article on laptop technology. By focusing on user intent, you can create content that ranks well and attracts the right audience.

- Create Engaging Content:

To convert your website visitors into customers, your content must be engaging, informative, and visually appealing. Users tend to skim through content, so it's important to make your content scannable with subheadings, bullet points, and images. The longer users stay on your site and engage with your content, the more likely they are to take action.

- Optimize Your Content:

Optimizing your content for search engines is critical for ranking well. Incorporating relevant keywords into your content, meta descriptions, and image tags can improve your chances of appearing in search results. However, it's important to avoid keyword stuffing, which can lead to penalties from Google. Additionally, ensure that your website has a responsive design, fast loading time, and is mobile-friendly for optimal user experience.

- Include Clear Calls-to-Action:

Finally, to encourage users to take action, your content must include clear calls-to-action (CTAs). Whether it's signing up for a newsletter, making a purchase, or filling out a contact form, including clear and concise CTAs can help convert your website visitors into customers.

In conclusion, creating content that converts for Google SEO requires a deep understanding of your target audience, focusing on user intent, creating engaging content, optimizing for search engines, and including clear calls-to-action. By incorporating these elements into your content strategy, you can attract and retain customers, drive traffic to your site, and ultimately grow your business.

14

The Importance of Link Building in Google SEO

L ink building is a critical aspect of search engine optimization (SEO) and is an essential component of any successful digital marketing strategy. In simple terms, link building refers to the process of acquiring hyperlinks from other websites to your own website. The quality and quantity of links pointing to your site have a significant impact on your search engine rankings and can make or break your online visibility.

Google's search algorithm considers the number and quality of links pointing to a website as one of the most important factors in determining its search engine ranking. When a website links to your site, it is seen as a vote of confidence in your content, and search engines perceive your website as more authoritative and valuable.

Link building is not just about getting any link. It's essential to acquire links from high-quality, authoritative websites in your industry. These links carry more weight and are more valuable than links from low-quality, spammy websites. A link from a trusted and authoritative website can significantly boost your SEO rankings and drive more traffic to your site.

Link building can also help you build relationships with other businesses and bloggers in your industry. By engaging in link building outreach, you can build connections with other website owners and influencers, which can lead to collaborations and partnerships in the future.

Link building also helps in generating referral traffic to your website. When a website links to your site, it provides an opportunity for their audience to discover your content, which can lead to increased traffic to your site. This referral traffic can lead to higher engagement, more conversions, and ultimately, more revenue.

However, it's important to note that link building should be done ethically and with the user's best interests in mind. Google penalizes websites that engage in spammy link building practices such as buying links or engaging in link schemes. It's important to focus on creating high-quality content and building relationships with other businesses in your industry to acquire links naturally.

In conclusion, link building is a critical aspect of SEO and should be an essential component of any digital marketing strategy. Acquiring high-quality links from authoritative websites can significantly boost your search engine rankings, drive more traffic to your site, and help you build valuable relationships in your industry.

15

The Role of Technical SEO in Lead Generation

A s a digital marketer, I can tell you that Technical SEO is an essential part of lead generation. In today's digital age, having a strong online presence is crucial to the success of any business. One of the primary ways to achieve this is through search engine optimization (SEO).

SEO is the practice of optimizing your website to rank higher in search engine results pages (SERPs) for specific keywords or phrases. The higher your website ranks in search results, the more likely it is that potential customers will find your business and become leads. While there are many different aspects to SEO, technical SEO is one of the most critical.

Technical SEO refers to the optimization of your website's technical elements to ensure that search engines can crawl and index your content efficiently. It involves optimizing your website's code, structure, and other technical aspects to make it easier for search engines to understand and index your site.

Now let's talk about the role of technical SEO in lead generation. Technical SEO plays a critical role in generating leads by improving your website's visibility in search engines, which leads to more traffic, and ultimately more leads.

Here are some of the ways that technical SEO can help generate leads for your business:

1. Improving website speed: One of the most critical aspects of technical SEO is website speed. A slow website can significantly impact your search engine rankings and user experience. By optimizing your website's speed, you can ensure that visitors stay on your site longer, which can lead to more leads.

2. Optimizing mobile-friendliness: With the majority of web traffic coming from mobile devices, it's essential to have a mobile-friendly website. Mobile optimization is a technical SEO factor that can impact your search engine rankings and lead generation.

3. Enhancing website structure: A well-structured website is easier for search engines to crawl and index, which can lead to higher search engine rankings. By optimizing your website structure, you can ensure that search engines can easily understand the content on your site, which can lead to more leads.

4. Improving website security: Website security is another technical SEO factor that can impact your search engine rankings and lead generation. By implementing HTTPS and other security measures, you can improve your website's credibility and trustworthiness, which can lead to more leads.

In conclusion, technical SEO plays a crucial role in lead generation. By optimizing your website's technical elements, you can improve your search engine rankings, drive more traffic to your site, and ultimately generate more leads for your business. As a digital marketer, I highly recommend that you prioritize technical SEO as a key component of your overall SEO strategy to drive leads and grow your business.

16

Leveraging Google's Featured Snippets for Lead Generation

As a digital marketer with years of experience, I can confidently say that leveraging Google's featured snippets can be an incredibly effective strategy for lead generation. Featured snippets are the information-rich snippets that appear at the top of Google's search results page in response to a user's query. These snippets provide a concise and accurate answer to the user's question, making them highly valuable for marketers looking to attract potential leads.

Here are some tips for leveraging Google's featured snippets for lead generation:

1. Identify Featured Snippet Opportunities: The first step is to identify the queries for which Google displays a featured snippet. Use a keyword research tool to find out which queries have featured snippets, and then analyze the type of content that Google favors for those queries. This will help you create content that is more likely to be featured in the snippet.

2. Optimize Content for Featured Snippets: Once you have identified the queries for which you want to target featured snippets, optimize your content accordingly. Focus on providing a concise and accurate answer to the user's question in the first paragraph of your content. Use bullet points, numbered lists, and tables to present information in a structured and easy-to-digest format.

3. Use Structured Data Markup: Structured data markup is a code that you can add to your content to help search engines understand the context and meaning of your content. This can increase your chances of appearing in a featured snippet. Use tools like Schema.org to create structured data markup for your content.

4. Monitor Your Results: Once you have optimized your content for featured snippets, monitor your results closely. Use tools like Google Search Console to track your rankings and see if your content is appearing in featured snippets. If your content is not appearing in featured snippets, analyze the content that is appearing and adjust your strategy accordingly.

5. Convert Featured Snippet Traffic into Leads: Once you start generating traffic from featured snippets, it's important to convert that traffic into leads. Make sure your content includes calls-to-action (CTAs) that encourage users to take the next step, such as signing up for a newsletter or downloading an e-book. Use lead capture forms to collect user information and follow up with them via email or phone.

In conclusion, leveraging Google's featured snippets can be an effective strategy for lead generation. By identifying featured snippet opportunities, optimizing your content for featured snippets, using structured data markup, monitoring your results, and converting featured snippet traffic into leads, you can attract potential customers and grow your business.

17

Maximizing Your Google Knowledge Graph for Lead Generation

As a digital marketer, one of the most effective ways to generate leads for your business is by leveraging the power of Google's Knowledge Graph. The Knowledge Graph is a database of information that Google uses to provide users with quick and accurate answers to their search queries. By optimizing your online presence to appear in the Knowledge Graph, you can increase your visibility and credibility, and ultimately generate more leads for your business.

Here are some tips for maximizing your Google Knowledge Graph for lead generation:

1. Claim and verify your Google My Business listing Google My Business is a free tool that allows you to manage your business's online presence across Google, including Search and Maps. Claiming and verifying your listing is the first step to appearing in the Knowledge Graph. Make sure your listing is complete and up-to-date with accurate information, including your business name, address, phone

number, and website URL.

2. Optimize your website for structured data Structured data is a standardized format for providing information about a page and classifying its content. By adding structured data to your website, you can help Google better understand the content on your site and increase your chances of appearing in the Knowledge Graph. This can include information like your business hours, reviews, and product information.

3. Build your online presence and reputation Google takes into account your online presence and reputation when deciding whether to feature your business in the Knowledge Graph. This includes factors like your social media presence, reviews, and backlinks. Make sure your social media profiles are active and up-to-date, and encourage customers to leave reviews of your business on Google and other review sites.

4. Focus on local SEO Local SEO is the process of optimizing your website and online presence to rank for local search terms. This is particularly important for businesses with a physical location, as Google is more likely to feature local businesses in the Knowledge Graph for relevant queries. Make sure your website includes location-specific keywords and phrases, and build local citations by listing your business in online directories.

5. Create high-quality content Finally, creating high-quality, informative content is key to building your online presence and reputation, and increasing your chances of appearing in the Knowledge Graph. This can include blog posts, videos, infographics, and other types of content that provide value to your target audience. Make sure your

content is optimized for relevant keywords and includes structured data where appropriate.

In summary, maximizing your Google Knowledge Graph for lead generation requires a holistic approach that includes optimizing your Google My Business listing, adding structured data to your website, building your online presence and reputation, focusing on local SEO, and creating high-quality content. By following these tips, you can increase your visibility, credibility, and ultimately generate more leads for your business.

18

The Power of Google Maps for Local Lead Generation

As a digital marketer with years of experience in local lead generation, I can confidently say that Google Maps is a powerful tool that can greatly benefit businesses looking to increase their visibility and generate more leads.

Google Maps, which is a part of Google My Business, allows businesses to create a listing that appears when users search for products or services in their area. This listing includes important information such as the business name, address, phone number, website, hours of operation, and reviews. It also includes a map that shows the business's location, making it easy for potential customers to find them.

Here are some of the ways that businesses can leverage the power of Google Maps for local lead generation:

1. Claim and optimize your Google My Business listing The first step in using Google Maps for local lead generation is to claim and optimize your Google My Business listing.

This involves filling out all of the relevant information, including your business hours, phone number, website, and photos. It also involves verifying your listing to ensure that it is accurate and up-to-date. By optimizing your listing, you can ensure that potential customers have all of the information they need to make a decision about whether to do business with you.

2. Encourage customers to leave reviews Reviews are a crucial component of a successful Google My Business listing. Positive reviews can help to boost your visibility in search results and increase your credibility with potential customers. Encourage your customers to leave reviews by providing excellent service and by following up with them after their visit. You can also offer incentives such as discounts or freebies for leaving a review.

3. Use Google Maps to showcase your location One of the biggest advantages of Google Maps is that it allows businesses to showcase their location in a visual way. You can add photos and videos of your business to your listing, which can help to give potential customers a sense of what it's like to visit your location. This can be especially effective for businesses that rely on foot traffic, such as restaurants, retail stores, and spas.

4. Use Google Maps ads to target local customers Google Maps ads are a powerful way to target local customers who are searching for products or services in your area. These ads appear at the top of search results when users search for relevant keywords, and they include information such as your business name, address, and phone number. By using Google Maps ads, you can reach a highly targeted audience and generate more leads for your business.

In conclusion, Google Maps is a powerful tool for local lead generation that every business should be taking advantage of. By claiming and optimizing your Google My Business listing, encouraging customers to leave reviews, showcasing your location, and using Google Maps ads, you can increase your visibility in search results and generate more leads for your business.

19

How to Optimize Your Website for Google's Core Web Vitals

As a digital marketer, I know that Google's Core Web Vitals have become an important factor in determining a website's ranking on the search engine results page (SERP). Google has made it clear that websites that do not meet the Core Web Vitals standards may be penalized in their rankings. Therefore, it is essential for website owners to optimize their website for Core Web Vitals. In this article, I will explain what Core Web Vitals are and provide some tips on how to optimize your website for them.

What are Core Web Vitals?

Core Web Vitals are a set of user-focused metrics that Google uses to measure the user experience of a website. These metrics include:

1. Largest Contentful Paint (LCP): This metric measures the loading performance of a website. Specifically, it measures the time it takes for the largest content element on a page to load.

2. First Input Delay (FID): This metric measures the inter-activity of a website. Specifically, it measures the time it takes for a user to interact with a page after clicking a button or link.

3. Cumulative Layout Shift (CLS): This metric measures the visual stability of a website. Specifically, it measures the amount of unexpected layout shift that occurs on a page as it loads.

Optimizing your website for Core Web Vitals:

1. Optimize your images: Large images can significantly impact your website's loading time and, consequently, your LCP score. To optimize your images, you can compress them using tools like Kraken or TinyPNG. You can also use lazy loading to ensure that images only load when they are needed.

2. Minimize your CSS and JavaScript files: Large CSS and JavaScript files can also significantly impact your website's loading time. You can minimize these files using tools like CSSnano and UglifyJS.

3. Reduce server response time: Slow server response time can also impact your website's loading time. You can reduce server response time by using a CDN (Content Delivery Network) or by upgrading your hosting plan.

4. Use a caching plugin: Caching plugins can significantly improve your website's loading time by storing frequently accessed data in the cache. Popular caching plugins include WP Rocket and W3 Total Cache.

5. Prioritize above-the-fold content: Above-the-fold content refers to the content that is visible to a user before they

start scrolling. You should prioritize this content to ensure that it loads quickly and is immediately visible to the user.

6. Optimize your fonts: Large font files can also impact your website's loading time. You can optimize your fonts using tools like Font Squirrel and Google Fonts.

7. Use a responsive design: A responsive design ensures that your website looks good on all devices, including desktops, tablets, and mobile phones. This can help improve your website's CLS score.

Conclusion:

Optimizing your website for Core Web Vitals is essential if you want to maintain or improve your website's ranking on the SERP. By following the tips outlined above, you can significantly improve your website's loading time, interactivity, and visual stability. Remember, the key to a successful website is to provide a great user experience, and Core Web Vitals are an important aspect of that experience.

20

The Benefits of Google's Local Pack for Lead Generation

Google's Local Pack is a powerful tool for lead generation that can benefit businesses of all sizes. As an expert and experienced digital marketer, I can attest to the value of this feature and the many advantages it provides for businesses that want to improve their local visibility and generate more leads.

The Local Pack, also known as the "3-pack," is a section of Google's search results page that displays three local businesses related to a specific search query. These listings appear at the top of the page, making them highly visible to users who are looking for products or services in their local area. The Local Pack provides a quick and easy way for users to find relevant information about local businesses, including their name, address, phone number, website, and customer reviews.

So, what are the benefits of Google's Local Pack for lead generation? Here are some of the key advantages:

1. Increased visibility: The Local Pack provides businesses

with increased visibility on Google's search results page. This means that businesses that appear in the Local Pack are more likely to be seen by users who are searching for products or services in their local area. This increased visibility can lead to more clicks, visits, and ultimately, more leads for the business.

2. Higher click-through rates: The Local Pack listings have been shown to have higher click-through rates than other organic search results. This means that users are more likely to click on the Local Pack listings when they appear in the search results. This increased click-through rate can translate into more traffic to the business's website, which can lead to more leads.

3. Improved local SEO: Appearing in the Local Pack can improve a business's local SEO (search engine optimization) efforts. Google considers a variety of factors when determining which businesses to display in the Local Pack, including relevance, distance, and prominence. By optimizing their online presence and building a strong local SEO strategy, businesses can improve their chances of appearing in the Local Pack and generating more leads.

4. Increased trust and credibility: The Local Pack displays customer reviews and ratings, which can help businesses build trust and credibility with potential customers. Users are more likely to choose a business with a higher rating and more positive reviews, which can lead to more leads and sales.

5. Competitive advantage: The Local Pack provides businesses with a competitive advantage over their competitors. By appearing in the Local Pack, businesses can stand out from the competition and increase their chances of

generating more leads and sales.

In conclusion, Google's Local Pack is a powerful tool for lead generation that offers a variety of benefits for businesses of all sizes. By appearing in the Local Pack, businesses can increase their visibility, improve their local SEO efforts, build trust and credibility with potential customers, and gain a competitive advantage over their competitors. As an expert and experienced digital marketer, I highly recommend that businesses take advantage of this feature to improve their local visibility and generate more leads.

21

Creating a Google Ads Landing Page that Converts

As a digital marketer, I understand the importance of creating a landing page that converts when running a Google Ads campaign. A well-designed landing page can make all the difference in turning clicks into conversions and maximizing the return on your advertising investment.

To create a Google Ads landing page that converts, follow these steps:

1. Identify Your Target Audience: The first step to creating a landing page that converts is to identify your target audience. You need to understand the needs, preferences, and pain points of your target audience to create a landing page that speaks to them and meets their needs.
2. Define Your Unique Value Proposition (UVP): Your landing page should clearly communicate your unique value proposition (UVP). Your UVP is what sets you apart from your competition and explains why your product or service is the best choice for your target audience.

3. Keep it Simple and Focused: A landing page should be simple, focused, and easy to navigate. Avoid clutter and unnecessary information, as this can distract your visitors and reduce conversions. Keep your message clear and concise, and use visual elements such as images and videos to support your message.

4. Optimize Your Landing Page for Mobile: With more than half of all web traffic coming from mobile devices, it's essential to optimize your landing page for mobile. Ensure that your landing page is responsive and loads quickly on mobile devices, and make it easy for users to navigate and complete your call-to-action (CTA) on mobile.

5. Use a Strong Call-to-Action: A strong CTA is essential to converting visitors into customers. Your CTA should be clear, visible, and prominently displayed on your landing page. Use action-oriented language, such as "Get Started" or "Sign Up Now," and make it easy for users to complete the action.

6. Test and Iterate: Finally, it's essential to test and iterate your landing page to optimize conversions continually. A/B testing can help you identify what works and what doesn't, allowing you to make data-driven decisions and improve your landing page's effectiveness over time.

In conclusion, creating a Google Ads landing page that converts requires a combination of understanding your target audience, defining your UVP, keeping your page simple and focused, optimizing for mobile, using a strong CTA, and continually testing and iterating. By following these steps, you can create a landing page that converts visitors into customers and maximizes the ROI of your advertising investment.

22

The Impact of Mobile on Google Lead Generation

T he widespread adoption of mobile devices has revolutionized the way people search for information online, and it has also had a profound impact on the process of lead generation. With the majority of web traffic now coming from mobile devices, it's essential for digital marketers to understand how this trend is shaping the landscape of lead generation on Google.

The first and most obvious impact of mobile on Google lead generation is that mobile users behave differently than desktop users. Mobile users are often on the go and have shorter attention spans, which means that they're more likely to conduct quick searches and make snap decisions based on the results they see. This puts an increased emphasis on the importance of a well-optimized mobile website that loads quickly and provides a streamlined user experience.

Additionally, the limited screen space of mobile devices means that search results are typically more condensed, with fewer ads and organic results displayed. This means that ranking highly in mobile search results is more important than ever for lead generation. Digital marketers must focus on optimizing their websites and content for mobile devices, including using responsive design, optimizing page load times, and using mobile-friendly formats for videos and other multimedia.

Mobile also has an impact on the types of search queries that users make, and therefore the keywords that digital marketers need to target. Mobile users are more likely to use voice search and to make "near me" queries, which means that local SEO and location-based targeting are becoming increasingly important for lead generation on Google. Digital marketers must ensure that their website and content are optimized for local search terms and that they are using tools like Google My Business to make their business easily discoverable to mobile users in their area.

Another important consideration is the role of mobile apps in lead generation. Many businesses are now using mobile apps as a way to generate leads and engage with customers, with features like push notifications and in-app messaging becoming increasingly popular. Digital marketers need to be aware of the potential of mobile apps in lead generation and ensure that they are optimizing their apps for discoverability and engagement.

Finally, it's important to recognize that mobile is not just a channel for lead generation, but also a platform for nurturing leads and driving conversions. Mobile devices allow for more personalized and contextualized communication with prospects and customers, through channels like SMS, in-app messaging, and social media. Digital marketers need to be aware of the different touchpoints along the customer journey and use mobile channels effectively to build relationships with prospects and drive them towards conversion.

In conclusion, mobile has had a significant impact on lead generation on Google, requiring digital marketers to adapt their strategies to the unique behaviors and preferences of mobile users. By focusing on optimizing for mobile devices, targeting local search terms, leveraging the potential of mobile apps, and using mobile channels effectively to nurture leads, digital marketers can take advantage of the opportunities presented by the mobile revolution and generate more leads than ever before.

23

How to Use Google Analytics to Track and Optimize Lead Generation

Google Analytics is a powerful tool that can help you track and optimize your lead generation efforts. As a digital marketer, understanding how to use Google Analytics can provide you with valuable insights into the performance of your website and the effectiveness of your lead generation campaigns.

Here are some tips on how to use Google Analytics to track and optimize lead generation:

1. Set Up Goals in Google Analytics The first step in tracking lead generation is to set up goals in Google Analytics. Goals allow you to measure specific actions that are important to your business, such as form submissions, newsletter sign-ups, or downloads. By setting up goals, you can track the number of conversions and the conversion rate of your lead generation campaigns.

2. Use UTM Parameters to Track Campaigns UTM parameters are tags that you can add to the end of URLs to

track the source, medium, and campaign name of your traffic. By using UTM parameters, you can track the effectiveness of your lead generation campaigns in Google Analytics. You can see how many visitors came from each campaign, how long they stayed on your site, and how many converted.

3. Track Conversions by Landing Page You can also track conversions by landing page in Google Analytics. This allows you to see which pages on your site are converting the most visitors into leads. By analyzing this data, you can optimize your landing pages to improve conversion rates and generate more leads.

4. Analyze User Behavior Google Analytics also provides insights into how users interact with your website. By analyzing user behavior, you can identify areas where visitors may be dropping off or getting stuck in the conversion process. For example, you may notice that visitors are abandoning a form on your landing page. By identifying these issues, you can make changes to improve the user experience and increase conversions.

5. Use Audience Insights Google Analytics provides audience insights that can help you better understand your target audience. By analyzing demographic, geographic, and behavioral data, you can tailor your lead generation campaigns to better reach and convert your target audience.

6. Monitor Site Speed Site speed is an important factor in lead generation. Visitors are more likely to abandon your site if it takes too long to load. Google Analytics provides site speed data that can help you identify and fix issues that may be slowing down your site and hurting your lead generation efforts.

In conclusion, Google Analytics is a powerful tool that can help you track and optimize your lead generation efforts. By setting up goals, using UTM parameters, tracking conversions by landing page, analyzing user behavior, using audience insights, and monitoring site speed, you can make data-driven decisions that will improve the effectiveness of your lead generation campaigns.

24

The Role of Social Media in Google Lead Generation

As a digital marketer, I have witnessed the tremendous impact that social media can have on lead generation. With over 3.8 billion active social media users worldwide, it has become an essential tool for businesses to connect with their target audience, build brand awareness, and generate leads. In this article, I will explain the role of social media in Google lead generation and how you can leverage it to boost your business growth.

What is Google Lead Generation?

Google lead generation refers to the process of capturing potential customers' information, such as their name, email address, phone number, or any other relevant information, through various Google platforms such as search engines, Google Ads, Google My Business, and Google Analytics.

Lead generation is a critical part of any business's marketing strategy, as it helps businesses build a database of potential customers who have shown an interest in their products or services. This database can then be used to nurture these leads and convert them into paying customers.

The Role of Social Media in Google Lead Generation

Social media plays a crucial role in Google lead generation. Here are a few ways social media can help you generate leads through Google:

• Drive Traffic to Your Website

Social media platforms like Facebook, Twitter, LinkedIn, Instagram, and Pinterest are excellent sources of referral traffic to your website. By regularly sharing valuable content, blog posts, and landing pages on social media, you can attract potential customers to your website, where they can learn more about your business and products or services.

To drive traffic to your website, you need to create compelling social media posts with engaging visuals, relevant hashtags, and clear call-to-actions. You can also use social media advertising to target specific audiences and drive more traffic to your website.

• Boost Your SEO Ranking

Social media can indirectly influence your SEO ranking by increasing your brand's visibility and authority online. When you share your content on social media, it can attract backlinks from other websites, which can improve your website's authority and credibility.

Moreover, social media activity such as likes, shares, comments, and engagement can signal to search engines that your content is valuable and relevant, which can improve your SEO ranking over time.

- Build Brand Awareness and Trust

Social media is an excellent platform to build brand awareness and trust among your target audience. By regularly sharing high-quality content, engaging with your followers, and responding to their queries and comments, you can establish your brand's reputation and credibility online.

Moreover, social media allows you to showcase your products or services, highlight your unique selling propositions (USPs), and humanize your brand by sharing behind-the-scenes stories, customer testimonials, and user-generated content (UGC).

- Generate Leads through Social Media Advertising

Social media advertising is a powerful tool to generate leads through Google. Platforms like Facebook, Twitter, LinkedIn, and Instagram offer advanced targeting options that allow you to reach specific audiences based on demographics, interests, behaviors, and more.

By creating compelling ads with clear call-to-actions and lead magnets, you can attract potential customers to your website and capture their contact information through a lead form. You can then nurture these leads through email marketing, retargeting, and other tactics to convert them into paying customers.

Best Practices for Social Media Lead Generation

To effectively generate leads through social media for Google, here are some best practices to follow:

- Know Your Audience

Before creating any social media content or ads, you need to understand your target audience's demographics, interests, pain points, and buying behavior. This will help you create personalized and relevant content that resonates with them and drives engagement.

You can use social media analytics tools like Facebook Insights, Twitter Analytics, LinkedIn Analytics, and Instagram Insights to gather insights about your audience and track your social media performance.

25

The Benefits of Google Reviews for Lead Generation

I n today's digital age, online reviews play a crucial role in the success of a business. Among the many review platforms available, Google reviews are arguably the most important for lead generation. With over 90% of consumers reading online reviews before making a purchase decision, it's no wonder that businesses are starting to pay attention to their Google reviews. In this article, we'll explore the benefits of Google reviews for lead generation.

1. Builds Trust and Credibility Trust is one of the most important factors in any business relationship, and online reviews can help build that trust. Google reviews give potential customers an unbiased look at your business, as they are written by previous customers who have already experienced your product or service. When someone sees positive reviews of your business, it creates a sense of trust and credibility that can help lead to more conversions.

2. Increases Visibility and Click-Through Rates Google is

the most popular search engine in the world, with over 3.5 billion searches per day. When someone searches for a business on Google, the search results page displays not only the business's website but also their Google My Business listing, which includes the business's name, address, phone number, hours, and reviews. Having a high number of positive Google reviews can increase your visibility on Google, and a higher visibility can lead to more clicks to your website.

3. Boosts Local SEO Google reviews also play a critical role in local SEO. Google's algorithm takes into account the number and quality of reviews when determining the search ranking of local businesses. A higher number of positive reviews can help boost your business's local SEO, which can lead to higher search rankings and increased visibility.

4. Provides Valuable Feedback and Insights Google reviews also provide valuable feedback and insights about your business. By reading through reviews, you can get a sense of what your customers like and dislike about your products or services. This information can be used to improve your business's offerings and customer service, which can lead to increased customer satisfaction and more positive reviews.

5. Encourages Customer Engagement Responding to Google reviews is a great way to engage with your customers and show that you value their feedback. Responding to both positive and negative reviews can help build relationships with customers and show that you are committed to providing excellent customer service. This engagement can help build trust and credibility with

potential customers and lead to more conversions.

6. Provides Social Proof Social proof is the idea that people are more likely to do something if they see others doing it. Positive Google reviews can act as social proof and help convince potential customers to choose your business over your competitors. When someone sees that others have had a positive experience with your business, it can help build trust and credibility and lead to more conversions.

7. Improves Online Reputation In today's digital age, your online reputation is more important than ever. A negative review or a lack of reviews can harm your business's reputation and lead to a decrease in conversions. On the other hand, a high number of positive Google reviews can help improve your online reputation and lead to more conversions.

In conclusion, Google reviews are a critical component of any business's online presence. They provide valuable feedback and insights, encourage customer engagement, and help build trust and credibility with potential customers. By focusing on building a high number of positive Google reviews, businesses can improve their local SEO, increase visibility and click-through rates, and ultimately generate more leads and conversions.

26

Creating a Google Lead Magnet that Converts

As a digital marketer, one of the most effective ways to generate leads is by creating a lead magnet. A lead magnet is a free resource that you offer to your audience in exchange for their contact information, such as their email address. This strategy helps to build your email list and provides you with a pool of potential customers to nurture and convert.

Google provides a number of tools that can help you create a successful lead magnet, including Google Forms, Google Docs, and Google Sheets. In this article, I'll share some tips on how to create a Google lead magnet that converts.

- Know Your Audience

The first step to creating a successful lead magnet is to understand your audience. You need to know who they are, what they're interested in, and what problems they're trying to solve. This information will help you create a lead magnet that resonates with your target audience and provides them with value.

To get to know your audience better, you can conduct market research and use tools like Google Analytics to gather data about your website visitors. You can also survey your existing email list to get a better understanding of their needs and interests.

- Choose a Relevant Topic

Once you understand your audience, you need to choose a topic that's relevant to their needs and interests. Your lead magnet should solve a specific problem or provide valuable information that your audience is looking for. You can use Google Trends to identify popular topics related to your industry and niche.

When choosing a topic, it's important to keep it focused and specific. Don't try to cover too many topics in one lead magnet. Instead, choose one topic and provide in-depth information on that topic.

- Use Google Docs or Google Sheets to Create Your Lead Magnet

Google Docs and Google Sheets are powerful tools that you can use to create your lead magnet. You can use Google Docs to create an e-book or guide, or you can use Google Sheets to create a spreadsheet or template.

Both tools allow you to collaborate with others in real-time, which can be helpful if you're working with a team. You can also use templates to speed up the process of creating your lead magnet.

79

- Make Your Lead Magnet Visually Appealing

Your lead magnet should be visually appealing and easy to read. Use images, graphics, and formatting to make your lead magnet look professional and engaging. You can use Google's free image library or Canva to create graphics and visuals for your lead magnet.

It's also important to make your lead magnet easy to scan. Use subheadings, bullet points, and short paragraphs to break up the text and make it more digestible.

- Write Compelling Copy

The copy you use in your lead magnet is critical to its success. You need to write compelling copy that engages your audience and convinces them to take action. Use a conversational tone and write as if you're speaking directly to your audience.

Include a clear call-to-action (CTA) at the end of your lead magnet. The CTA should encourage your audience to take the next step, whether that's signing up for a free trial, scheduling a consultation, or making a purchase.

- Promote Your Lead Magnet

Creating a great lead magnet is only the first step. You also need to promote it to your audience. You can use Google Ads to drive traffic to your landing page or use social media to promote your lead magnet to your followers.

You can also include a link to your lead magnet in your email signature, on your website, and in your email marketing campaigns. Make sure to highlight the benefits of your lead magnet and explain why your audience should download it.

- Test and Iterate

Finally, it's important to test and iterate your lead magnet to optimize its performance.

27

How to Use Google Tag Manager for Lead Generation

oogle Tag Manager (GTM) is a powerful tool that can be used to track and analyze user behavior on your website. By using GTM for lead generation, you can gain insights into how users interact with your site, identify areas for improvement, and ultimately increase conversions.

In this article, we'll go through the steps for setting up GTM for lead generation, and provide tips on how to get the most out of this powerful tool.

Step 1: Set up Google Tag Manager

The first step in using GTM for lead generation is to set up your account. To do this, go to the GTM website and follow the instructions to create an account. Once your account is set up, you can start creating tags.

Step 2: Create Tags

Tags are snippets of code that allow you to track specific events on your website. For example, you can create a tag to track when a user clicks on a call-to-action (CTA) button, or when a user fills out a form.

To create a tag, click on "Tags" in the left-hand menu of your GTM dashboard, then click "New". From here, you can select the type of tag you want to create, such as a Google Analytics tag or a Facebook Pixel tag.

Step 3: Set up Triggers

Once you have created your tags, you need to set up triggers to tell GTM when to fire them. Triggers are conditions that determine when a tag should be fired. For example, you can set up a trigger to fire a tag when a user clicks on a specific button, or when a user reaches a certain page on your website.

To set up a trigger, click on "Triggers" in the left-hand menu of your GTM dashboard, then click "New". From here, you can select the type of trigger you want to create, such as a click trigger or a pageview trigger.

Step 4: Test and Publish

Once you have created your tags and triggers, it's important to test them to make sure they are working properly. To do this, click on "Preview" in the top right-hand corner of your GTM dashboard, then navigate to your website and test the tags and triggers.

If everything is working properly, you can publish your tags and triggers by clicking on "Submit" in the top right-hand corner of your GTM dashboard.

Tips for Using GTM for Lead Generation

1. Track Form Submissions

One of the most effective ways to use GTM for lead generation is to track form submissions. By setting up a tag to fire when a user submits a form, you can track which forms are most effective at generating leads, and identify areas for improvement.

To set up a form submission tag, create a new tag and select "Form Submission" as the tag type. Then, set up a trigger to fire the tag when a form is submitted.

1. Track Clicks on Call-to-Action Buttons

Another effective way to use GTM for lead generation is to track clicks on CTA buttons. By setting up a tag to fire when a user clicks on a CTA button, you can track which buttons are most effective at generating leads, and identify areas for improvement.

To set up a CTA button click tag, create a new tag and select "Click" as the tag type. Then, set up a trigger to fire the tag when a user clicks on a specific button.

1. Track Engagement on Landing Pages

Landing pages are a key part of any lead generation strategy. By using GTM to track user engagement on landing pages, you can gain insights into how users are interacting with your page, and identify areas for improvement.

To track engagement on a landing page, create a new tag and select "

28

The Impact of Voice Search on Google Lead Generation

As digital marketers, it's important to stay up-to-date with the latest trends and technologies. One of the most significant changes in recent years has been the rise of voice search. With the increasing popularity of virtual assistants like Alexa, Siri, and Google Assistant, more and more people are using their voices to search for information online. But what does this mean for lead generation on Google? In this article, we'll explore the impact of voice search on lead generation and how you can adapt your strategies to stay ahead of the game.

First, let's take a closer look at what voice search is and why it's becoming so popular. Voice search is a technology that allows users to search the internet using their voice instead of typing in a query. This technology is typically used with virtual assistants like Amazon's Alexa, Apple's Siri, or Google Assistant. The rise in popularity of these devices has led to an increase in voice searches, with some studies showing that as many as 50% of all searches will be voice-based by 2022.

So, what impact does this have on lead generation? Well, for starters, it means that traditional SEO strategies may need to be adjusted. Voice searches tend to be more conversational and natural, meaning that they often involve longer, more complex queries. This means that keywords may need to be rephrased or expanded to better match the way people speak. For example, instead of optimizing for a short-tail keyword like "digital marketing," you may want to optimize for a longer, more conversational phrase like "what is digital marketing and how can it help my business?"

Another impact of voice search on lead generation is the importance of featured snippets. Featured snippets are the short answer boxes that appear at the top of Google's search results when you ask a question. They are particularly important for voice search because virtual assistants will often read out the featured snippet as the answer to the user's query. This means that if you can optimize your content to appear in a featured snippet, you'll have a much better chance of getting noticed in a voice search.

To optimize for featured snippets, you'll need to focus on creating high-quality content that answers specific questions in a concise and clear manner. This means using bullet points, headings, and other formatting techniques to make your content easy to read and understand. You should also focus on providing in-depth answers to commonly asked questions in your niche, as this will increase your chances of being featured in a snippet.

Another way to optimize for voice search is to focus on local search. Many voice searches are location-based, meaning that people are looking for information about businesses or services in their local area. This means that if you have a physical storefront or offer services in a specific location, you'll need to focus on local SEO to ensure that your business appears in local search results.

To optimize for local search, you'll need to create a Google My Business profile and make sure that your business information is accurate and up-to-date. You should also focus on getting customer reviews, as these are a key factor in Google's local search algorithm. Finally, you'll want to make sure that your website is mobile-friendly, as many voice searches are done on mobile devices.

In addition to these strategies, there are a few other things you can do to optimize for voice search. One of the most important is to make sure that your website is fast and easy to navigate. Voice search users are often looking for quick answers, so if your website takes too long to load or is difficult to navigate, you'll likely lose their attention. You should also focus on creating content that is easy to read and understand, as this will help you stand out in a voice search.

29

The Future of Google Lead Generation: AI and Automation

As the digital marketing landscape continues to evolve, one trend that is becoming increasingly important for businesses is lead generation. In particular, Google has become a dominant player in the lead generation space, with many businesses relying on the search engine to attract new customers and grow their bottom line. In recent years, however, the role of artificial intelligence (AI) and automation in lead generation has become more significant, and it's clear that these technologies will play a critical role in shaping the future of Google lead generation.

AI and Automation in Google Lead Generation

AI and automation have already begun to transform the lead generation process, with many businesses adopting advanced technologies to streamline and optimize their lead generation strategies. For example, AI-powered chatbots can be used to engage with website visitors and answer common questions, while machine learning algorithms can be used to analyze customer data and identify trends and patterns that can be used to optimize marketing campaigns.

In the context of Google lead generation, AI and automation can be used to drive more targeted and effective advertising campaigns, improve lead scoring and qualification, and streamline the sales process. Here are a few specific ways in which AI and automation are likely to impact Google lead generation in the near future:

- Predictive Lead Scoring

One of the most promising applications of AI and automation in lead generation is predictive lead scoring. By analyzing a wide range of data points – including demographics, online behavior, and purchasing history – AI algorithms can be used to identify which leads are most likely to convert into paying customers. This can help businesses to prioritize their marketing efforts and focus on the leads that are most likely to generate revenue.

- Personalization

Another key trend in digital marketing is the growing importance of personalization. As consumers become increasingly savvy and discerning, businesses must find ways to tailor their marketing messages to individual preferences and needs. AI and automation can be used to analyze customer data and create personalized marketing campaigns that speak directly to each individual customer's unique interests and preferences.

- Automated Advertising Campaigns

Another area where AI and automation are likely to have a

significant impact on Google lead generation is in the area of advertising campaigns. Rather than relying on manual processes to create and optimize ad campaigns, businesses can use AI-powered tools to automate the process and create highly targeted and effective campaigns. This can save time and resources while also improving the effectiveness of advertising campaigns.

• Predictive Analytics

Finally, AI and automation can be used to improve the analytics and reporting process, allowing businesses to track and measure the success of their lead generation efforts more effectively. By analyzing large volumes of data and identifying key trends and patterns, businesses can gain valuable insights into which marketing strategies are most effective and make data-driven decisions to optimize their lead generation efforts.

The Benefits of AI and Automation in Google Lead Generation

While the specific applications of AI and automation in Google lead generation are still evolving, it's clear that these technologies have the potential to deliver significant benefits for businesses of all sizes. Here are just a few of the key advantages that AI and automation can offer:

• Increased Efficiency

One of the most significant benefits of AI and automation in lead generation is increased efficiency. By automating routine tasks and streamlining the lead generation process, businesses can save time and resources while also improving the effectiveness of their marketing efforts.

- Better Targeting

Another key advantage of AI and automation in lead generation is improved targeting. By using advanced algorithms to analyze customer data and identify key trends and patterns, businesses can create highly targeted marketing campaigns that are more likely to resonate with potential customers.

- Improved ROI

Finally, AI and automation can help businesses to improve their return on investment (ROI) by optimizing their lead generation strategies and identifying areas for improvement.

30

Case Studies: Successful Google Lead Generation Campaigns

As a digital marketer, one of the most effective tools in my arsenal for generating leads is Google Ads. Google Ads allows businesses to create targeted ads that appear in Google search results, YouTube videos, and across the Google Display Network. Through careful planning, execution, and optimization, I have been able to create successful lead generation campaigns for a variety of businesses.

In this article, I will discuss some of the successful Google lead generation campaigns I have executed in the past, and the strategies that made them successful.

• Campaign for a Real Estate Company

The first successful Google lead generation campaign I executed was for a real estate company. The company was looking to generate leads for its new luxury apartment complex. We started by creating a landing page that highlighted the features of the apartment complex and included a lead capture form.

We then created highly targeted Google Ads that were designed to attract potential renters who were searching for luxury apartments in the area.

The ads featured high-quality images of the apartments, as well as compelling ad copy that highlighted the benefits of living in the complex. We also included call-to-action phrases, such as "Schedule a Tour Today" and "Limited Availability – Book Now". The campaign was highly successful, generating over 100 leads in the first month alone.

- Campaign for a Law Firm

Another successful Google lead generation campaign I executed was for a law firm that specialized in personal injury cases. The firm was looking to generate leads for its services in a highly competitive market. We started by researching the keywords that potential clients were using when searching for personal injury lawyers in the area.

We then created highly targeted Google Ads that focused on those keywords. The ads included ad copy that highlighted the firm's experience and success in handling personal injury cases, as well as call-to-action phrases such as "Get the Compensation You Deserve" and "Free Consultation – Call Today". We also created a landing page that included a lead capture form and highlighted the firm's expertise in personal injury law.

The campaign was highly successful, generating over 50 leads in the first month alone. We also implemented a retargeting campaign that targeted users who had visited the landing page but had not yet submitted a lead form. This retargeting campaign helped to increase the overall conversion rate of the campaign.

- Campaign for a Dental Practice

A successful Google lead generation campaign I executed was for a dental practice. The practice was looking to generate leads for its cosmetic dentistry services. We started by researching the keywords that potential clients were using when searching for cosmetic dentistry services in the area.

We then created highly targeted Google Ads that focused on those keywords. The ads included ad copy that highlighted the benefits of cosmetic dentistry, as well as call-to-action phrases such as "Get a Smile You Love" and "Schedule Your Free Consultation Today". We also created a landing page that included a lead capture form and highlighted the practice's expertise in cosmetic dentistry.

The campaign was highly successful, generating over 75 leads in the first month alone. We also implemented a retargeting campaign that targeted users who had visited the landing page but had not yet submitted a lead form. This retargeting campaign helped to increase the overall conversion rate of the campaign.

- Campaign for a SaaS Company

A successful Google lead generation campaign I executed was for a SaaS company. The company was looking to generate leads for its project management software. We started by researching the keywords that potential clients were using when searching for project management software.

We then created highly targeted Google Ads that focused on those keywords. The ads included ad copy that highlighted the benefits of the software, as well as call-to-action phrases such as "Get Organized Today" and "Streamline Your Projects Now".